NEW JERSEY

W9-BLH-012

Marlton Pike

Cooper River

HADDONFIELD

70

130

CAMDEN

676

Walt Whitman Bridge

GLOUCESTER CITY

Independence Hall

F.D. Roosevelt Park

76

Sch...

Penrose Ave.

291

Fort Mifflin

River

WOODBURY

Mantua Creek

PITMAN

45

2

1

0

Distance in miles

New Jersey Tpke.

130

295

13

Island Ave.

Philadelphia International Airport

Delaware

PAULSBORO

DARBY

MacDade Blvd.

Chester Pike

...Ave.

95

N

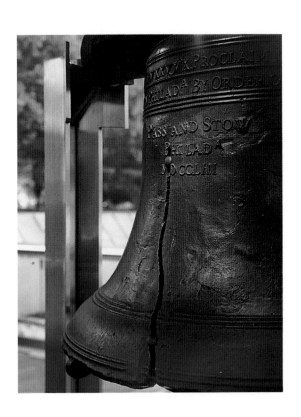

CAROL M. HIGHSMITH AND TED LANDPHAIR

PHILADELPHIA

A PHOTOGRAPHIC TOUR

CRESCENT BOOKS

NEW YORK

THE AUTHORS WISH TO THANK THE FOLLOWING FOR THEIR GENEROUS
ASSISTANCE IN CONNECTION WITH THE COMPLETION OF THIS BOOK:

Dennis B. Arwood and Craig R. Baclit, Elliott-Lewis Company
Julie P. Curson, Philadelphia
Pamela and David Dembe, Philadelphia
Eve and David Eagan, Jenkintown
Meryle Fischer, Philadelphia Convention and Visitors Bureau
Don and Lynn Martin Haskin, Philadelphia
Rosemarie and Marc Kuhn, Plantation, Florida
Joyce and Robert Mozenter, Chestnut Hill
Hyman Myers, Philadelphia
J. Mickey Rowley, Top of the Tower
John Todd, Chestnut Hill
Robert Williams, Pennsylvania Convention Center Authority

————

This 1998 edition is published by Crescent Books®,
an imprint of Random House Value Publishing, Inc.,
201 East 50th Street, New York, N.Y. 10022.

Crescent Books® and colophon are registered trademarks of
Random House Value Publishing, Inc.

Random House
New York • Toronto • London • Sydney • Auckland
http://www.randomhouse.com/

Printed and bound in China

Library of Congress Cataloging-in-Publication Data
Highsmith, Carol M., 1946–
Philadelphia / Carol M. Highsmith and Ted Landphair.
p. cm. — (A photographic tour)
Includes index.
ISBN 0-517-18615-2 (hc: alk. paper)
1. Philadelphia (Pa.)—Tours. 2. Philadelphia (Pa.)—Pictorial works. I. Landphair, Ted, 1942–
II. Title. III. Series: Highsmith, Carol M., 1946– Photographic tour.
F158.18.H54 1998   97–39858
917.48´110443´0222—dc21   CIP

8 7 6 5 4

————

Project Editor: Donna Lee Lurker
Designed by Robert L. Wiser, Archetype Press, Inc., Washington, D.C.

All photographs by Carol M. Highsmith unless otherwise credited:
map by XNR Productions, page 5; Philadelphia Museum of Art, the Mr. and Mrs. Wharton Sinkler
Collection, oil painting, page 6; Urban Archives Center, Temple University, pages 8, 15, 17, 18, 21;
Historic Society of Pennsylvania, pages 9–11, 13, 14, 16; Prints and Photographs Division,
Library of Congress, pages 12, 20; The Frank Weer Collection page 19

FRONT COVER:
Independence Hall,
once the state house of
Pennsylvania and site
of the signing of the
Declaration of Inde-
pendence, is the cen-
terpiece of Philadel-
phia's Independence
National Historical
Park. BACK COVER:
According to a story
that some scholars
dispute, George Wash-
ington asked Betsy
Ross, a Philadelphia
upholsterer, to design
the first United States
Flag, and she stitched
the Stars and Stripes
in her modest Society
Hill home. PAGE 1:
The Liberty Bell, cast
in 1751 to mark the
fiftieth anniversary
of William Penn's
Charter of Privileges
for the Pennsylvania
Colony, cracked
during testing, was
recast, then cracked
again. PAGES 2–3: The
skyline of "colonial"
Philadelphia has
changed dramatically
in recent years.

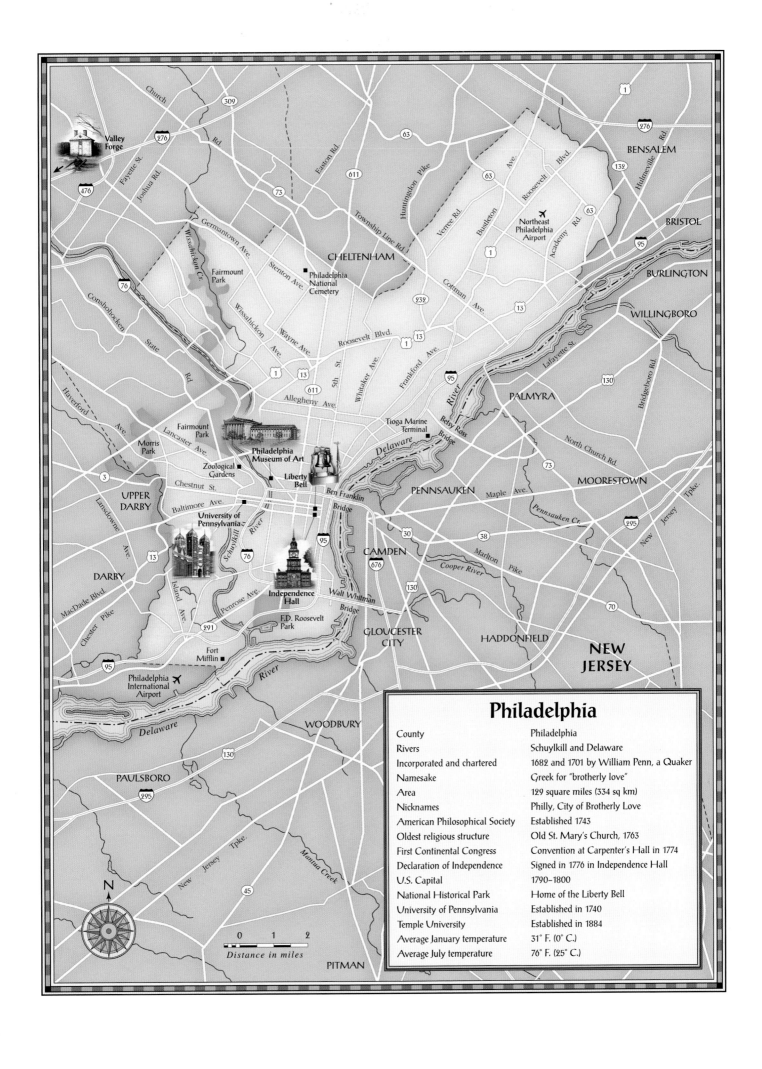

Philadelphia

County	Philadelphia
Rivers	Schuylkill and Delaware
Incorporated and chartered	1682 and 1701 by William Penn, a Quaker
Namesake	Greek for "brotherly love"
Area	129 square miles (334 sq km)
Nicknames	Philly, City of Brotherly Love
American Philosophical Society	Established 1743
Oldest religious structure	Old St. Mary's Church, 1763
First Continental Congress	Convention at Carpenter's Hall in 1774
Declaration of Independence	Signed in 1776 in Independence Hall
U.S. Capital	1790–1800
National Historical Park	Home of the Liberty Bell
University of Pennsylvania	Established in 1740
Temple University	Established in 1884
Average January temperature	31° F. (0° C.)
Average July temperature	76° F. (25° C.)

CHANGE? PAROCHIAL OLD PHILADELPHIA? Who would have thought that after three centuries of mostly minding its own business, the hard-working industrial city of narrow streets, grimy factories, and quaint colonial buildings would be transformed almost overnight into one of America's most dynamic and appealing tourist destinations? Anyone who had visited the nation's birthplace fifteen years ago, perhaps to see Independence Hall or Valley Forge, and had not returned until now would hardly recognize it. Invigorated by a sleek new skyline and revitalized waterfront, an exploding arts scene, and a profusion of incredible restaurants, clubs and sporting events, Philadelphia has shed its inferiority complex and blossomed into the Paris of America. And why not? Its tree-lined, flag-festooned Benjamin Franklin Parkway, connecting City Hall with the Philadelphia Museum of Art—with the Rodin Museum and one of seven copies of Rodin's famous *The Thinker* statue midway at Logan Circle—was designed by French landscape architect Jacques Greber with the Champs Elysées in mind. In the mid-1990s, the city of William Penn, Benjamin Franklin, and John James Audubon enhanced its historic core, dressed up its verdant squares and parks—including the largest landscaped municipal park in the nation—remodeled picturesque train stations and marketplaces, and turned the boundless energy of a man whom media everywhere dubbed "America's mayor" into a tidal wave of optimism and physical renewal.

Although the birthplace of the United States of America grew to become the nation's greatest manufacturing center, Philadelphia was often overlooked in the roll call of great American cities. Part of the reason was its proximity to New York, less than one hundred miles away. New York had a bigger harbor right on the ocean, soaring skyscrapers—at a time when a gentleman's agreement kept Philadelphia buildings lower than "Billy Penn's hat" atop City Hall—and most important, the world's most ambitious publicity and media machines. Television networks covered Philadelphia out of New York or Washington, and even Philly's own newspapers often ignored positive local developments unless they had first been reported in the *New York Times*. Cities like New Orleans, Seattle, and Memphis—each a fraction the size of Philadelphia but blessed by being the dominant city of a region—promoted their charms, got individualized media attention, and raked in tourists and their dollars. Boston, with one-third Philadelphia's population and no greater historic heritage or grander city parks, could hardly handle the crowds, while Philadelphia contented itself making locomotives, lace, and lasagna. Tourists stopped in Philadelphia, of course, just long enough to visit Independence Hall. But they rarely stayed. There was too much to see and do in New York, Baltimore, Washington, and the Pennsylvania Dutch country. Philadelphia hotels were stopovers for traveling business and sales people, and survived only by hosting weddings, graduation dances, and other local events.

But Philadelphia had more than the curse of proximity to New York and other Northeast tourist centers to blame for its introversion. It was "the Quaker City," after all, the "greene Countrie Towne" founded by William Penn. Even though this heritage was mostly a historical curiosity by the 1900s, self-effacing Quaker attitudes, such as frowning on ostentation and self-promotion, endured. No one should stand out, so Philadelphia did not try. Penn named his New World city "Philadelphia"—Greek for "City of Brotherly Love"—but its latter-day reputation as a gruff, blue-collar town, a place where even Santa Claus was once booed unmercifully at an Eagles' football game, held it back. Word of the city's incredible educational resources or cultural diversity did not always spread beyond the Delaware River. "We arrived

Benjamin West's Benjamin Franklin Drawing Electricity from the Sky hangs at the Philadelphia Museum of Art. The inventive "Dr. Franklin," as he was known around town, experimented with lightning in his quest to better fireproof buildings. This "humble printer," as he called himself, published Poor Richard's Almanack under the pseudonym "Richard Saunders."

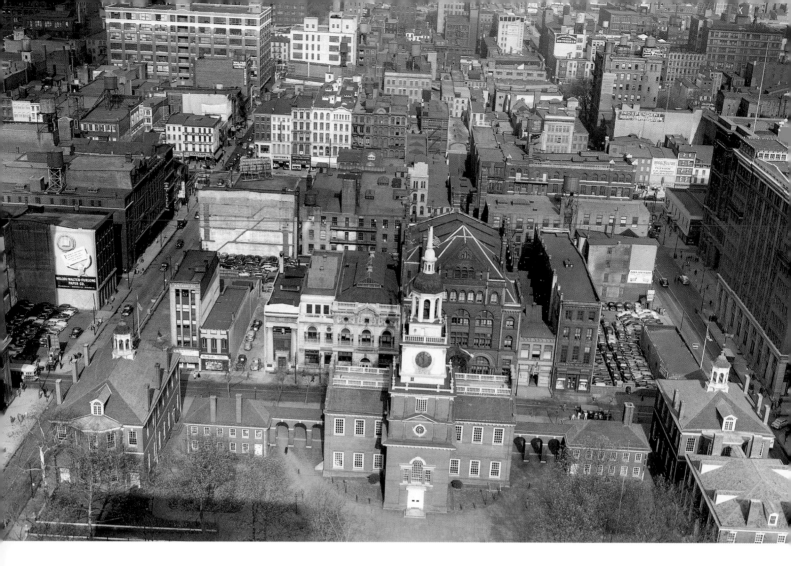

in Philadelphia on Sunday," veteran broadcast journalist Jack Smith once observed, "but it wasn't open." Stage and film comic W. C. Fields suggested as his epitaph, "On the whole, I'd rather be in Philadelphia," meaning even a stay in the plebian city he had often lampooned in his vaudeville routines beat the alternative he'd be facing on his deathbed.

Because many of Philadelphia's neighborhoods had once been independent towns—with distinct industries, ethnic makeup, dress, and even accents and expressions—its politicians perfected ward politics and spoils and rarely cared what the outside world thought about it. Executives of most of the giant manufacturing companies concerned themselves with profits, not civic chauvinism. Many important decisions were finalized over cigars and brandy at private clubs. Writer John Gunther called them "an oligarchy more compact and more entrenched than any in the United States." No one was in much of a hurry; projects like a new city hall or performing-arts center would often take twenty or more years to agree upon and get going, with the result that the end product sometimes seemed old-fashioned the day it opened.

That was then, in an earlier, provincial time. But now is a time of electrifying change in Billy Penn's town.

The area between the Delaware River and a smaller stream, the Skuylkill River, was occupied by Lenni Lenape Indians when Swedes and Finns, spreading north from New Sweden in present-day Delaware, first settled in the area in the 1640s. Then it was briefly Dutch after Peter Stuyvesant, governor of New Netherlands, based on Manhattan Island, seized the area. But Britain's King Charles II, whose agents already had a foothold in the New World in Virginia, ignored Dutch claims and granted the entire region to his brother, the Duke of York. The English booted Dutch officials out of Manhattan without firing a shot and set about expanding their hold on the Mid-Atlantic Region. On March 14, 1681, Charles granted most of what is today Pennsylvania to William Penn, as payment of a large debt owed Penn's father by the Duke of York. The younger Penn was a member of the Society of Friends—the Quakers—and he viewed the charter as an opportunity to conduct a "holy experiment" in the utopian New World by establishing a colony that would welcome settlers of all faiths.

Penn journeyed to "Pennsylvania"—Penn's Woods—only twice, staying two years during his longest visit. His agents faced no Indian resistance, for the Lenni Lenapes, by then called Delawares, were as much pacifists as the Quakers. Penn's surveyor, Thomas Holme, laid out the colony's dream city in a strict grid pattern, interrupted by squares and small parks, that would be copied in hundreds of American towns in the future. Most of the original houses were made of brick, kilned from red river-bottom clay. The original twelve-hundred-acre town was only a few blocks deep, ranging between Vine Street on the north, South Street to the south, and the two rivers on the east and west. These would remain the city's boundaries until 1854, when thirteen surrounding townships in Philadelphia County were consolidated into the city. Penn actively advertised for colonists in England, Holland, and Germany, and he soon attracted a diverse mix of Quakers, Anglicans, Presbyterians, and Catholics. Even Jews, shunned in many other colonies, were welcomed. Although its harbor was far up the Delaware, Philadelphia prospered as an entrepôt for timber, furs, and farm products from the fertile Pennsylvania countryside. And because Penn actively recruited shipbuilders, glassmakers, wheelwrights, and silversmiths, skilled crafts got a strong foothold in the city.

Even in 1910 there was a market for antiques and folk art—staples of the Old Curiosity Shop on Pine Street. Antique shops are still a fixture in the neighborhood.

Benjamin Franklin, a brilliant and eccentric inventor, publisher, scientist, diplomat—and wit—who moved to Philadelphia from Boston in 1723 at age seventeen to work as a journeyman printer, dominated the scene for sixty years to follow. Franklin was city postmaster and founder of the college that became the Ivy League's University of Pennsylvania. In his bicentennial history of Pennsylvania, Thomas C. Cochran noted that Franklin's *Poor Richard's Almanack*, which he edited under the pseudonym "Richard Saunders," reached a circulation of 10,000 and became, "next to the Bible, the most universally seen book in the colonies." His barbed aphorisms, such as, "He that lieth down with dogs shall rise up with fleas," read as true today as they did when he wrote them. The Junto Club that Franklin founded was the first of many "social benefit societies" in town; through the club, he proposed what later became the first circulating library in America. And it was the droll Franklin who, when John Hancock urged unanimous adoption of Thomas Jefferson's Declaration of Independence in 1776, signaled his agreement to the assembled Continental Congress by saying, "We must indeed all hang together, or most assuredly we shall all hang separately."

On the eve of the American Revolution, Philadelphia was the second-largest English-speaking city in the world, and the leading city in Britain's worldwide colonial empire. When disagreements between the North American colonies and Britain turned violent, it was to Carpenters' Hall in Philadelphia that twelve colonies sent delegates to the First Continental Congress in 1774. But revolution was not on the minds of the delegates. While there were calls for civil disobedience to emphasize the degree of the colonists' displeasure with restrictive

British taxes and tariffs, reconciliation was the goal. After the battles of Lexington and Concord in Massachusetts, however, a Second Continental Congress was convened in 1775 in the Pennsylvania State House. In that building, which would become known as Independence Hall, George Washington was named commander-in-chief of a continental army. War became a virtual certainty after nearly one thousand British soldiers were killed or wounded at the Battle of Bunker Hill in Charlestown, outside Boston. In July 1776 in Philadelphia, Thomas Jefferson quickly drafted a Declaration of Independence that, when adopted, committed the colonists to an irrevocable fight for freedom from British rule. Although the city was pivotal to the drive for independence, many prosperous Philadelphia merchants remained loyal to the crown, and thousands of pacifist Quakers refused to fight as well. After defeating colonial forces at Brandywine Creek, Paoli, and Germantown, British troops under General William Howe occupied Philadelphia in September 1777. The Continental Congress fled to Lancaster and then to York, Pennsylvania, and the State House's "Liberty Bell" was hauled to safety in Allentown. Meanwhile, General Washington and his troops endured a terrible winter at Valley Forge to the west of town.

The British were not decisively defeated until 1781 at Yorktown, Virginia, but thousands of Tory loyalists were long gone from Philadelphia by that time. They had departed with British troops three years earlier. As the new nation struggled to get organized, a Philadelphian, Robert Morris, a Liverpool-born merchant who was one of the signers of the Declaration of Independence, organized the Bank of North America to help pay the government's war debts. The bank established Philadelphia as the nation's financial center. At first the new United States was a loose conglomeration of states that finally got organized with the

The soaring 547-foot tower of Philadelphia's new City Hall had just been completed in Center City when this phototype was produced. Until 1909, it was the world's tallest masonry-bearing structure.

drafting of a federal constitution at Independence Hall in 1787. George Washington was inaugurated as the first president in New York City two years later, and in 1790 the capital was moved from New York to Philadelphia—just in time for newcomers to face a terrible yellow fever epidemic that killed one-tenth of Philadelphia's population. The capital remained in Philadelphia for almost ten years before being moved to a permanent federal enclave called "Washington," along the Potomac River, in 1800.

New York overtook Philadelphia as the nation's largest and most dominant city soon thereafter. New York benefitted from its deep-water port and its location at the mouth of the Hudson River, down which goods from the heartland flowed after traversing the Erie Canal. Philadelphia responded by extending the Pennsylvania Railroad through the Alleghenies, but New York countered with the westward extension of its own New York Central. As Pennsylvania's population fanned out along the rail line, the state capital moved to centrally located Harrisburg in 1812.

In 1894, the statue of William Penn— the work of Alexander Milne Calder and John Casani—was about to be hoisted to its perch atop City Hall's tower. "Billy Penn" soon became a favorite symbol of the city and its people.

As Philadelphia slipped as a government and financial center, it ascended industrially to become the "Workshop of the World" and the hub of America's Industrial Revolution. For more than a century, Philadelphia was the nucleus of America's textile, apparel, machining, furniture, boiler, and shipbuilding industries. Saws, gears, rugs, streetcars, hose, and handbags by the millions—and uncounted tons of sugar and flour—poured out of twenty thousand Philadelphia plants and mills at the turn of the century. The city was blanketed in black soot from billowing smokestacks and locomotives. The giant Baldwin works—Philadelphia's largest employer in the years before World War I—turned out thousands of locomotives right in the heart of Center City. Cramp and Sons built ships for the Union during the Civil War, in which a Philadelphian, General George Gordon Meade, was the hero of the decisive Battle of Gettysburg. Cramp also built the battleship *Maine*, whose sinking in Havana harbor ignited the Spanish-American War. Philadelphia's J. G. Brill Co. became the world's largest maker of streetcars, cable cars, and trolleys. In the Tacony neighborhood, the Disston Saw Works produced countless giant saw blades. Even the famous "ten gallon" Stetson hats were made, not in Texas, but in the Kensington section of Philadelphia. Ten Philadelphia firms made pianos or organs. A "Brewerytown" complex of five local breweries grew up near Baker Bowl, home of the Philadelphia Phillies baseball team in North Philadelphia. The American League Philadelphia Athletics—the legendary team of owner-manager Cornelius McGillicuddy, known as Connie Mack—had its own stadium, Shibe Park, not far away. Clothing was often fabricated in sweatshops, then lugged to people's homes in Jewish and Italian neighborhoods, where women finished the trimming and added buttons. During World War I, American International Shipbuilding created the nation's largest shipyard at "Hog Island" on the south edge of town.

All the while, immigrants poured in from Italy, Poland, and Russia, settling along the Delaware River and in outlying neighborhoods like Manayunk and Frankford. Once the breadwinner was employed, some immigrant families rarely left their neighborhoods. Why should they? The job was nearby, the language of the Old Country was spoken on the streets and in church and barber shops and pool halls, there were newspapers in that language readily available, and social clubs

In 1916 Broad Street was hopping at night, though it does not appear there was much room for passing autos once theatergoers had found spots on the street for their roadsters.

made the newcomers feel welcome. Hearing that there were jobs, blacks from the American South arrived in droves as well. In response to the influx of strangers, many long-time Philadelphians moved outward to pleasant suburbs, especially after streetcars were electrified in the 1890s.

Ten million visitors toured the big Philadelphia Centennial world's fair in 1876, in which a massive Corliss engine—manufactured, however, in Providence, Rhode Island—was the star attraction. It provided power for the entire fair, and hundreds of other drill, lathe, press, and saw manufacturers from throughout the nation displayed their wondrous machines as well. By then, railroad tracks and railyards of the Pennsylvania, Philadelphia & Reading, and Baltimore & Ohio lines were everywhere in town. The Pennsy even built an incredible stone viaduct, carrying several tracks from its station near City Hall west across the Skuylkill. Locals called it "the Chinese Wall." By 1910, Philadelphia produced goods in 80 percent of the 264 categories of manufactured articles listed by the Bureau of the Census. Unlike Pittsburgh—the "Steel City"—Akron (tires), or Detroit (automobiles), no one industry dominated the Philadelphia economy. This helped level out economic peaks and valleys, but it also meant the city grew at a less spectacular pace. Amazingly in so industrial a city, there were more than two hundred farms inside city limits as late as 1940.

Philadelphia became the "City of Homes"—usually owner-occupied rather than rental—because so many workers lived practically next door to their factories or office buildings. Italians gravitated to South Philadelphia, blacks at first to West Philadelphia and then north of downtown, Jews to Northeast, Irish and Ukrainians to Kensington, Poles to Manayunk and Chester, "WASPS" to Chestnut Hill and Germantown. Until streetcars and trolleys spread north and west of town, commuters were a rarity. In 1894, when the massive City Hall was topped off, more than one hundred thousand Philadelphians still lived in Center City. The wealthy walked to their banks and offices from Rittenhouse Square and other fashionable streets nearby. Neighborhood boundaries were undeclared yet surprisingly rigid; Philadelphia's Chinatown, for instance, unlike those in most other big cities, did not spread appreciably beyond a few blocks around Vine Street. So distinctive are neighborhood dialects to this day that locals can tell whether a West Philadelphian is from the "tops" or the "bottoms"—the wealthier higher-numbered addresses or the working-class lower end. Kensington prides itself on being "Rocky's neighborhood" from the smash movie series of *Rocky* movies about a Philly boxer who makes it big. The films lionize Philadelphians' grit and determination, as when Sylvester Stallone, as Rocky Balboa, bounds up the steep Museum of Art steps and raises his hands in a salute to his anticipated victory. "Yo, Rocky," shout supporters as he passes.

"Yo" is an all-purpose Philadelphia greeting. "Naydiv tawk," Philadelphia columnist Clark DeLeon calls it. "It's more than an accent, it's an attitude," he writes. "Or, as we pronounce it, addytood." Other words that DeLeon says visitors can practice in "Fluffya":

Kwawfee—"The liquid stuff that keeps cab drivers going."

Purdy—"The view of the Senda Ciddy skyline out the windas."

Youse—"Second person singular."

Yiz—"Second person plural."

South Philadelphia, with its five-block-long Italian Market full of fresh produce, cheeses, fish and squid, skinned rabbits, and a hundred other delicacies, remains Philadelphia's most idiosyncratic neighborhood. It, too, has its own stereotypes—what Murray Dubin, author of a book on South Philly, calls "13-year-old girls with big hair or tough guys in tee-shirts named Tony." The city's first ethnic ghetto when Irish dock workers and their families crowded into the Southwark section, South Philadelphia today offers some of the nation's best, yet most unpretentious, Italian restaurants. Over the years, it has produced a wealth of celebrities, from Frankie Avalon and Bobby Rydell to Eddie Fisher, Toots Shor, and Marian Anderson. Man Ray, the international artist and photographer, grew up in South Philadelphia. So did Larry Fine of the Three Stooges, and Chubby Checker, who turned "the Twist" into a national obsession. To this day there is a South Philadelphia museum honoring the great opera singer Mario Lanza, who once drove a bus in town. South Philly is the neighborhood from which the funloving Mummers spring. The Mummers strut down Broad Street in outrageous sequined and feathered costumes on New Year's Day, to their string bands' rendition of "O' Dem Golden Slippers." There are several stories about the origin of their name. One has it deriving from the expression, "Mum's the word," since most Mummers parade silently. Another traces it to the German word *Mumme*, for "mask." Still another ties Mummers to Momus, the Greek god of censure and mockery. Now the various Mummers' clubs have their own museum on Washington Avenue on the edge of South Philadelphia.

Many Philadelphians of all races and from every part of the region personify "Rocky's" gruff exterior and warm heart. They respect others who also work hard and have little patience for those who put on airs. Their athletic heroes are the unassuming, everyday players, not the

Whole new neighborhoods of row houses with tiny front porches—a step up for many families— edged into farmland in the first decade of the twentieth century. Here, the elevated train ran down Sixty-ninth Street.

supercilious superstars who flaunt their fat contracts and coast through games. "Philadelphians open to you like fine wine breathes," says longtime Philadelphia newspaper columnist and banking executive Don Haskin. "They open to you the longer they get to know you."

Literally hundreds of thousands of two- and three-story row houses were constructed all across the city. Politicians and Philadelphia's strong unions made sure of it. They worked to see that everyone who wanted one had a good-paying job and a house to go home to. As a result there were few New York-style tenements or Chicago-type "apartment cities." Even in middle-class suburbs like Mount Airy, row houses outnumbered detached duplexes or single-family homes. Except for corner units, which were designed to accommodate stores or shops, floor plans were identical. Only an occasional awning broke up the monotony of stoops and window treatments extending to the horizon. Many units were surprisingly spacious. But others were little more than shanties, packed back to back against other rows of houses, with only tiny backyards and an alley in between. Row houses could be easily converted into storefront cheese, poultry, fish, and produce markets—with the owner and his family living upstairs. Pushcarts and sidewalk bazaars filled with wagons, open sacks, and barrels added even more color. Neighbors kept an eye on each other's children; celebrated births, mourned deaths, and attended church or temple together; and threw block parties at the slightest provocation. Fittingly, when U.S. cities were invited to show off examples of their progress at the great World's Columbian Exposition in Chicago in 1893, Philadelphia sent a single-family row house.

Since 1894, Center City has been dominated by the massive Second Empire-style City Hall. It was then that Alexander Milne Calder's statue of William Penn—still the largest single piece of sculpture atop any building in the world—was completed. City Hall, which was the grandest and most expensive public building in the world—costing the equivalent of three billion in today's dollars—was unusual in that it was designed to house the city administration, council, and municipal courts. It is home to the Pennsylvania Supreme Court, the oldest judicial body in North America, which also meets in Harrisburg and Pittsburgh. City Hall's placement was remarkably faithful to Penn's 1682 Plan for Philadelphia; it was built on precisely the spot, filling the intersection of Broad and Market Streets, that Penn had intended for public buildings two hundred years earlier. With its completion, the locus of Center City moved westward, away from the river and William Penn's old town. Even the block-long Bourse building at Fifth and Chestnut streets—base of the financial community, including the maritime, stock, and grain exchanges—was left behind by the westward march of progress.

Office towers, including the Central Penn National Bank, Provident Mutual Life Insurance, and Fidelity Bank buildings, rose in 1928, only to see the onset of the Great Depression a year later following the stock-market crash. As Frederic Miller, Morris Vogel, and Allen Davis point out in *Still Philadelphia*, their photographic history of the half century leading up to World War II, "When the PSFS Building, downtown's most architecturally important skyscraper, was opened at 12 South 12th Street in 1932, local citizens joked that its sign meant "Philadelphia Slowly Faces Starvation." None of these buildings rose beyond the 548-foot height of Billy Penn's hat. Philadelphia trained its own "Philadelphia School" of architects like Frank Furness and Robert

Similar neighborly scenes, as captured in this 1946 photograph, which the Philadelphia Record *entitled "Sociability on Summer Street," can still be found on hundreds of Philadelphia blocks today.*

Venturi and gave them plenty of work designing practical buildings utilizing "functional expressionism"—meaning that buildings were rarely disguised or gussied up. They looked like what they were to be used for: a school like a school, a factory like a factory, and so forth. Less is not more in urban architecture, Venturi once said. "Less is a bore." Philadelphia had the resources to import a McKim, Mead and White; a Skidmore Owings and Merrill; a Mies van der Rohe; or other out-of-town masters. But unlike Chicago or New York, it rarely bothered to until late in the twentieth century.

Near City Hall stood the city's two colossal train terminals—the Pennsy's Broad Street Station, and the Reading Terminal with its gigantic indoor food market. Wanamaker's Department Store filled half a block on Market Street, and other dry-goods stores like Lit Brothers', Gimbel's, and Strawbridge and Clothier's located nearby as well. After Gimbel's inaugurated radio broadcasting in the city when WIP signed on in 1922, most of the other stores did likewise, advertising their wares. Women and children made a day of shopping downtown. Friends would "meet at the eagle"—a six-foot-high bronze bird at the center of Wanamaker's first floor. A "must" excursion for residents from throughout the region was a Christmastide trip downtown to see the animated displays in department-store windows and the model-train exhibit that wound through Wanamaker's first floor. Every imaginable variety of small shop existed within a few blocks. Photos from the early twentieth century show such concerns as "Parisian Pleating & Novelty Co.," "Dr. J. F. Mitchell—Foot Specialist's" office, a Horn and Hardart lunchroom (its "automats" would abound around town later), a billiards hall, and a United cigar shop. In one photo, a sign above a dentist's office reads, "BE SURE you get in the right office. There are lots of FAKERS practicing dentistry in this neighborhood." A tenderloin district, complete with movie, burlesque, and minstrel houses, "menagerie" museums, and tawdry hotels offering twenty-five-cent rooms, was a popular part of Center City.

Trolleys and their overhead power lines ultimately covered more than eighty routes and six hundred miles of track throughout the city and suburbs. Ironically the trolleys and commuter rail lines helped bring the city together, but they also increased the isolation of the economic classes and spurred the development of separate "streetcar suburbs" farther and farther from downtown. Surface transit competed with autos for rights of way through the city's crowded streets, and trolleys were eventually phased out on all but a few routes by subways, elevated lines, or buses.

Philadelphia ultimately declined as an industrial center. The Great Depression of the 1930s took a terrible toll on small companies and craft shops in particular. Cramp's Shipyard shut down; so, many years later, did the government's Navy Shipyard. These closures alone cost the city more than ten thousand jobs. Layoffs at Baldwin Locomotive Works, Midvale Steel, and other big companies were followed by downsizing, relocation, or closings later. Manufacturing rebounded briefly during World War II, when Philadelphia again became a key component of the Arsenal of Democracy. Baldwin switched to making tanks, Disston Saw crafted armor plate, and Brill turned from making trolleys to producing gun carriages. But it was a last gasp. The labor-intensive machinery at many plants was hopelessly obsolete

In early 1946 everything was in readiness in the Kensington neighborhood for the return of boys from the front following the end of World War II. Residents organized a banquet and gave each serviceman a $125 check.

for meeting the sophisticated challenges ahead. Immediately after the war, strikes against several big companies soured the city's labor climate as well. Many mills and factories closed for good, and others moved to the nonunion South. Thousands of workers departed with them, and others left the city for dream homes in suburban enclaves like Levittown, a mass-produced housing development in lower Bucks County modeled after the Levitt Company's experimental community on Long Island. In the 1950s alone, the population of the seven counties ringing Philadelphia more than tripled, to 2.3 million. Left behind, especially in North Philadelphia below Lehigh Avenue, was a notorious black slum. What had been the nation's third-largest city—more populous than Los Angeles—in 1950 lost half a million people in the four decades to follow. While some plants did retool, and newer industries like pharmaceutical manufacturing and petroleum refining emerged, Philadelphia would miss out on the microchip and computer revolutions that invigorated Boston and several Sun Belt cities' economies.

Under reform mayor Joseph Clark in the 1960s, the city waded into urban renewal, tearing down the Pennsy's Chinese Wall and replacing it with a stretch of office buildings called Penn Center; reclaiming the Society Hill neighborhood, which included the mansion used by presidents Washington and Adams, from a slum into a model neighborhood of colonial townhouses; cleaning up the area around Carpenter's Hall and Todd House—Dolley Madison's childhood home—constructing a park and pedestrian mall around Independence Hall, and walling-in gardens and building walkways among other historic structures.

Except for the popularity of Philadelphia musicians and a television teenage dance show called "Bandstand" that soon began a long network run, the nation seemed to lose sight of

Philadelphia. That changed, however, in 1971 with the election of Frank Rizzo as mayor. Rizzo, a policeman's son who was himself a former police commissioner, bulled his way into one confrontation and national headline after another. Former mayor Clark called him "Philadelphia's Mussolini" after one of Rizzo's crackdowns on black protesters, and there was a concerted effort to recall the blunt-spoken mayor. But Rizzo survived. One of the low points for the city's national image occurred in 1978 with the fiery destruction of the headquarters of MOVE, a largely black radical cult, in West Philadelphia. Thirteen MOVE members and one police officer died in the confrontation. Milder-mannered William J. Green Jr. succeeded Rizzo in 1979, and Green's managing director, Wilson Goode, in turn succeeded him, beating back another Rizzo challenge.

But the election of Edward G. Rendell in 1992, when Philadelphia was teetering on the edge of bankruptcy, sparked a change for the better in Philadelphia's outlook and image. The upbeat Rendell, a New Yorker who had attended the University of Pennsylvania and stayed, got not just his adopted city, but also the rest of the nation, talking about the "New Philadelphia." On nationwide radio and television talk shows and in hundreds of print interviews, he extolled the entire nine-county region that spills into northern Delaware and southern New Jersey. "Comeback City," *Holiday* magazine called Philadelphia in 1995. "The sky's the limit for a confident Philadelphia." When *Forbes* listed America's best cities for business in 1996, Philadelphia was third. "From its bustling downtown to its numerous historic sites," wrote Cox News Service in a story distributed across the nation, "Philadelphia can compete with almost anything Europe has to offer." "The nation's friendliest city," *Condé Nast Traveler* magazine called Philadelphia.

Philly had long been the brunt of an old joke: What's the difference between Philadelphia and yogurt? Yogurt has culture. But in 1996, *USA Today* lauded Philadelphia's artistic renaissance. "Today the city is alive with culture, visual art, music, theater and dance," the paper gushed. This, after Rendell pinpointed South Broad Street as the "Avenue of the Arts" and got the ball rolling on a new concert hall and new theaters there. Rendell ticked off nationally renowned cultural attractions, including the Philadelphia Orchestra (which has sold more recordings than any other orchestra in the world), the Franklin Institute science museum, the Opera Company of Philadelphia, the Pennsylvania Academy of the Fine Arts, the Afro-American Historical and Cultural Museum, the American Swedish Historical Museum, and the Barnes Foundation Gallery, all of which—with the help of discounted hotel/arts packages—have made Philadelphia a must-stop for "cultural tourists." Proof came in 1996, when the touring Cézanne Exhibition, making its only U.S. stop at the Philadelphia Museum of Art, drew tens of thousands of visitors and generated an estimated $86.5 million for the city. Of course the art museum's building itself, designed by Horace Trumbauer and built over twelve years beginning in 1916, is an attraction. It is actually three temples, two serving as wings to the main section, reached from the Benjamin Franklin Parkway by a prodigious flight of stairs flanked by cascading fountains.

Each spring, the "Olympics of Gardening"—the Philadelphia Flower Show—attracts more than 250,000 visitors from around the world. Even though Philadelphia had been called the "Athens of

You can expect the unexpected at the New Year's Mummers' Parade. In 1922, Frank Focacci of the League Island Club was all arms and legs—eight of them!

America" in the nineteenth century, contemporary Americans were only just discovering institutions like the Curtis Institute, one of the world's top musical training schools, or the Settlement Music School, the nation's largest community school of arts, which began as a place where immigrant children could get piano lessons for a nickel. Almost without notice, parts of Old City near the Delaware River had become Philadelphia's own SoHo—a district of artists' lofts and galleries, architects' studios, and lively clubs.

But just as important to the bruised psyche of the city as his "New Philadelphia" campaign to all who would listen outside of town, Rendell walked the streets, shaking hands and raving about Philadelphia to the citizens themselves. "America's mayor" showed up unexpectedly at the smallest neighborhood meetings and embraced business and civic leaders from throughout the region. At one gathering, he astonished the audience by totalling the attendance at all of the hundreds of Philadelphia Phillies baseball, Flyers hockey, Eagles football, 76ers basketball, and Spirit soccer games from the previous year and pointing out that Philadelphia's museums drew more visitors. Another time, he noted that Greater Philadelphia has more colleges and universities—eighty-two—not even mentioning the seven medical schools in the region, than the Boston and Baltimore areas combined. The nation's top-rated business school—Wharton at the University of Pennsylvania—is located in Philadelphia, and the region awards more than ten thousand academic degrees each year in the sciences, health care, and medical technology; 3,400 in engineering, 1,300 in computer science; and 3,000 at the masters level in business administration.

Outdoor markets have long been part of the rhythm of Philadelphia. Many a household saves its shopping for fruits, vegetables, poultry, and pasta for a trip to South Philadelphia's Italian Market.

No one discovering or re-discovering Philadelphia could fail to notice Liberty Place, whose twin towers broke the old, unwritten height restrictions for downtown buildings. Developer Willard G. Rouse hired Chicago architect Helmut Jahn to design the sixty-story, Art Deco One Liberty Place, whose blue glass, neon trim, and lancet crown are reminiscent of Manhattan's Chrysler Building. It and its fifty-eight-story companion tower, Two Liberty Place, invigorated the Philadelphia skyline.

Lower to the ground, but high in the esteem of nostalgic Philadelphians, is the restored

Reading Terminal, which has been modernized and converted into the East Coast's second-largest convention center. Along with it, the colorful old terminal market below the old train concourse has been cleaned and modernized. From its train shed and head house office tower on East Market Street, Philadelphia & Reading commuter trains had streaked northwest through Germantown and Chestnut Hill toward the coal town of Reading, and northeast as far as Jersey City, New Jersey. For ninety-one years, from 1893 to 1984, an estimated eight million Philadelphians commuted to and from Center City on the Reading to work or shop. A pleasant midday diversion was a walk to the Reading Terminal Market for lunch and grocery shopping. For years the Reading Railroad even carried bags of groceries to suburban stations and held them there, for free, while families continued their marketing. After it turned decrepit, the historic terminal was saved from the wrecker's ball by the Pennsylvania Convention Center Authority, which purchased the property and proceeded to convert it into a massive, state-of-the-art convention facility, a limestone, glass, and granite showplace that retained subtle reminders of the old train shed.

S HEAD. RDG TERMINAL.

"It has been changed from a gritty piece of municipal infrastructure to a glittering symbol of a post-industrial city," wrote Thomas Hine in the *Philadelphia Inquirer*.

Another fascinating example of innovative restoration involves the building that once housed the city's grandest hotel, the 1904 Bellevue Stratford. From the moment Prussian immigrant George Boldt opened the 1,094-room French Renaissance-style hotel in 1904 with the biggest bash in city history, it was the center of social and political life in Philadelphia. A stay at the Bellevue was deliberately modeled after a pampered journey on an ocean liner. All the leading clubs that did not own their own buildings met there. But as the century wore on, the hotel, like other old downtown hostelries nationwide, lost its luster, so the owners hid its great columned portico behind glass and aluminum, obscured the lobby's soaring coffers under a drop ceiling, and replaced overstuffed and inlaid furniture with blond, laminated pieces. "Old in Grace, New in Face," trumpeted its owners. Occupancy slid, and there were rumors that it would close even *before* a hotelier's nightmare struck. Within a month of getting home from a week of U.S. bicentennial festivities in 1976, 182 American Legion members became violently ill; twenty-nine died. All had stayed at the Bellevue Stratford. While it would be shown that this "Legionnaires' Disease," contracted from bacteria in the mists of cooling units, drinking fountains, and shower heads, had shown up in other hotels worldwide as well, the outbreak at the Bellevue Stratford doomed the hotel. After limping along nearly empty, it closed on November 18, 1976. Seven months later, Rubin Associates, a developer of shopping centers and office buildings, bought the hotel for $8.25 million—about what it had cost to build—and embarked upon a $25-million rehabilitation directed by Hyman Myers. But occupancy figures remained weak: there simply were not enough high-end travelers to Philadelphia at the time to fill the

Virtually every one of the tracks was occupied in the early years of the old Reading Terminal. This was most likely a Friday afternoon, when not only commuters but also vacationers to the Poconos boarded trains.

19

city's several new luxury hotels. So Rubin Associates reassessed and undertook a second restoration, also designed by Myers, costing four times as much as the first. The building then reopened as a retail and office tower, topped by a smaller, 170-room hotel, the Hotel Atop the Bellevue. Ironically, harking back to the Bellevue Stratford's days of ocean-liner attentiveness, its new management firm was the Cunard Company.

Of course, Old Philadelphia is as charming as ever, and Independence Hall and the Liberty Bell remain its magnet. The bell, which was moved out of Independence Hall into its own enclosure to mark the nation's bicentennial in 1976, was originally ordered from England to celebrate the fiftieth anniversary of William Penn's Charter of Privileges. Before it could be hung in the belfry of the State House, someone tried it out, and it cracked. Two local workers recast it, and the bell was hung in 1753. It rang many times over the next few years but may have stood silent on July 8, 1776, when the Declaration of Independence was proclaimed. That's because the State House belfry was rotting, and there was fear that ringing the bell would bring it crashing down. In subsequent years the Liberty Bell developed another crack—made worse by well-intended "repairs," to the point that it became entirely symbolic rather than functional.

Other popular downtown sites include Elfreth's Alley in Old City, the oldest continuously occupied street in America; the giant U.S. Mint; the restored Bourse building; and the house where Elizabeth Griscom "Betsy" Ross, a local seamstress, may (or may not) have designed the first Stars and Stripes flag of the new nation following the Declaration of Independence. Great churches are everywhere. Among the most historic are the 1700 Gloria Dei—also called Old Swedes'—Lutheran Church, the oldest church in Pennsylvania, and other eighteenth century churches, including Old Pine Street (Presbyterian), St. Peter's (Episcopal), Old St. Mary's and Old St. Joseph's (Roman Catholic), and Mother Bethel (African Methodist Episcopal).

Also decidedly *not* new in Philadelphia is its tasty "street food"—including "Philly

In 1933 as now, the skyline view from the high ground of the Philadelphia Museum of Art is one of the best in town. This is the Great Depression year that unemployment hit its peak in Philadelphia.

COPYRIGHT · 1933
PHOTO·ILLUSTRATORS

cheesesteak" hoagies, hot pretzels and chestnuts vended from steaming carts, and tomato bread—a deep-dish pizza without cheese or toppings. That's not to forget scrapple, a pasty brick made from the scraps left after the slaughter of hogs. Locals call it "Philadelphia paté." So who would have guessed that Philadelphia would land seven of America's Top 50 restaurants, including Nos. 1 and 2, in *Condé Nast Traveler's* 1994 readers' poll?

The Philadelphia area is laced with beautiful homes, many made of stone, that sell for as little as a third the cost of comparable homes in other big American cities. Philadelphians are fifty-five minutes from the Atlantic Ocean; one and one-half hours from the Pocono Mountains; fifty minutes from the big Atlantic City gambling resort; a stone's throw from Revolutionary War battlefields, Pennsylvania Dutch inns and restaurants, and Bucks County antique shops; and minutes from a sail on the Delaware or Skuylkill rivers. Their 8,900-acre Fairmount Park—named for Faire Mount, the hill atop which the Philadelphia Museum of Art sits—boasts not only the expected athletic fields and woodsy vistas but also more than two hundred pieces of outdoor sculpture, including works by Frederic Remington and Auguste Rodin.

Local deejay Dick Clark was twenty-seven when he took over Bandstand *in 1956. To the dismay of parents, the show enthralled teenagers, and a year later Clark went national with* American Bandstand.

Downtown in what are called "special services districts"—where business people pay an extra city fee to keep the grounds clean, bright, and safe—visitors are liable to encounter a costumed character in a three-cornered colonial hat, passing out pamphlets about nearby attractions and nightlife. The absence of a museum—anywhere in the United States—to explain and celebrate the U.S. Constitution and Bill of Rights was addressed when Congress chartered a nonpartisan organization charged with building a new Constitution Center family destination on Independence Mall. The announcement called for exhibits, films, live theater, children's galleries, and interactive materials on the Internet's World Wide Web, particularly during the week beginning on Constitution Day, September 17, each year. Fundraising of the more than $150 million needed to make the center a reality by its target opening date of Constitution Day, 2000, began in the mid-1990s and was modeled after the wildly successful public-private effort that resulted in the refurbishing of the Statue of Liberty and Ellis Island's visitor center.

Recognizing that Philadelphia had fallen behind other, more aggressive metro areas in attracting and supporting businesses, Greater Philadelphia First, an organization of chief executives of Philadelphia-area companies, began a regionwide effort to improve public schools, strengthen technical training programs, and attract new corporations in "clusters" such as data-intensive services, hospitality, and health care. In the last category alone, Greater Philadelphia First pointed out, metro Philadelphia already ranked second-largest in health education and research, with 123 hospitals and clinics, including twenty-four teaching hospitals, plus multiple schools of dentistry, nursing, pharmacology, and veterinary medicine. It ticked off the score of pharmaceutical houses and hundreds of biotech research centers in the area, but also pointed to subtler advantages of the Philadelphia region—like a seven-minute rapid-transit ride from the Greater Philadelphia Airport to Center City office buildings and hotels.

Philadelphia is smaller but stronger than it was a half-century ago. It's still tinkering with its mix of modern and historic, cultured and brash. But it's certainly not disheartened any longer, and the joke is on anyone who underestimates the City of Brotherly Love.

OVERLEAF: Fanlights grace the doorways of many Federal-style Society Hill townhouses, such as the 1815 Philip Syng Physick House. Physick—the city's leading surgeon of the period—and other physicians at the Pennsylvania Hospital turned Philadelphia into the nation's pre-eminent center of medical education.

PHILIP SYNG PHYSICK
FATHER OF
AMERICAN SURGERY
LIVED IN THIS HOUSE
1815 - 1837
RESTORED IN HIS MEMORY
AND
AS AN EXAMPLE OF A
RESIDENCE OF THE FEDERAL PERIOD
BY
THE PHILADELPHIA SOCIETY
FOR THE PRESERVATION OF LANDMARKS

The Department of the Interior erected a postmodernist "ghost" structure (above) to mark the spot in Center City where Benjamin Franklin built his three-story house and print shop. Beneath "Franklin Court" is the Franklin Museum, whose exhibits recount many of the eclectic interests of the city's most famous "Renaissance man." In 1775, the Second Continental Congress convened in Independence Hall (right), the Pennsylvania Colony statehouse. A year later, delegates adopted the Declaration of Independence and appointed George Washington commander-in-chief of the Continental Army. It was to Independence Hall, too, that the founders returned to draft and approve the constitution for the new nation in 1787.

Elfreth's Alley (opposite), created in 1703, is the nation's oldest continuously occupied street. Row houses, which appeared in the late eighteenth century, were occupied primarily by local craftsmen. Jeremiah Elfreth, for whom the alley is named, was a blacksmith. Wealthier business investors in the Pennsylvania Colony lived in Society Hill townhouses. Major David Lenox, president of the Bank of the United States, occupied this 1759 house (left) on Spruce Street. Later, government leaders lived in Society Hill when Philadelphia was the nation's capital. The neighborhood, close to Independence Hall, declined during Philadelphia's industrial boom and was a slum by the 1950s when "urban renewal" targeted the area. By the 1980s, Society Hill had regained its cachet. I. M. Pei was among the architects who designed towers and townhouses in the revitalized neighborhood.

Samuel Blodgett Jr.'s 1797 First Bank of the United States (left) was commissioned by Secretary of the Treasury Alexander Hamilton soon after the nation adopted a single currency. William Strickland designed the Merchant's Exchange (above)—the first stock exchange in the country. After the exchange dissolved during the Civil War, vendors kept food stalls around the building for more than a century. Bookbinder's Restaurant (overleaf), which opened in 1865 and became the restaurant of choice of Philadelphia and visiting celebrities, is now a landmark. "Booky's," as some natives call it, is famous for its soups. The family sold this original Bookbinder's in the 1940s and opened Bookbinder's Seafood House on South Fifteenth Street.

29

The Smythe Stores building (opposite), constructed in stages at Front and Arch streets between the mid-1800s and early 1900s, is one of the best remaining examples of cast-iron design in Philadelphia. Once a department store, the building is now a condominium. Gloria Dei, or "Old Swedes'," Church (left and above), dedicated in 1700, is Philadelphia's oldest church building. Swedes settled in present-day Wilmington, Delaware, and colonized an area from Trenton to the mouth of the Delaware Bay. The history of "New Sweden" is traced elsewhere at Philadelphia's American Swedish Historical Museum.

B'nai Brith commis-
sioned Moses Ezekiel's
Religious Liberty
statue (above) for the
U.S. Bicentennial in
1976. It was dedicated
in Fairmount Park but
in 1986 was moved to
the National Museum
of American Jewish
History. Philadelphia
Architecture *calls the
1727 Christ Church
(right) "the most
sumptuous building in
the colonies." So many
patriots and loyalists
worshiped together at*
*the principal Anglican
Church in Quaker
Philadelphia that it
became known as "the
nation's church." Leg-
endary Philadelphia
Orchestra conductor
Eugene Ormandy is
among the luminaries
buried in the Old Pine
Street Church grave-
yard (opposite). The
1766 Presbyterian
church was a hospital,
and even a stable,
under British occu-
pation during the
Revolutionary War.*

THE GAMEWELL JOKER

If you were to send an alarm from the box at Independence Hall, which is numbered "1776", it would be registered on the "Gamewell Joker" system you see here. The box would send a series of electrical taps to this system. A single tap, a pause, then seven more taps, pause, seven taps, pause and six taps, indicating the number 1776.

The house gong would ring out the taps and they would also be registered on the proper tape. A quick glance at the "run" board in the center and firefighters would know if they were to respond and where.

When this firehouse was active, it is said certain fire horses could recognize the signals from the "Joker" and

The Fireman's Hall Museum (left) is located in the 1876 Engine Company No. 8 firehouse on Second Street. Benjamin Franklin (who else?!) organized the city's first fire company in 1736, and in 1871 the city's volunteer groups merged into the nation's first professional fire department. Among the museum's displays is the "Joker" fire alarm system. The exhibit is wired in such a way that visitors will hear today's fire alarms as they would throughout the city. Head House Square (above) was Society Hill's new market when it opened in 1745. Vendors rented spaces, first from a private company, then from the city, which took over the operation in 1772. Volunteer firefighters used some of the houses as stations, and fire companies met upstairs to socialize.

When Paul Philippe Cret's Benjamin Franklin Bridge (above) spanned the Delaware River in 1926, it was the largest suspension bridge in the world. The commuter route to suburban New Jersey has also become a dazzling light sculpture. For the U.S. Bicentennial, architect Steven Izenour designed a system—still in use—that illuminates each of the bridge's cables at night. The lights follow the progress of passing trains. The USS Olympia (opposite), docked at the Independence Seaport Museum at Penn's Landing, was Admiral George Dewey's flagship at the decisive Battle of Manila Bay during the Spanish-American War. Its final task was to ferry the body of the nation's Unknown Soldier home to Arlington National Cemetery in 1921. Mothballed U.S. Navy ships (overleaf) are berthed at the Philadelphia Naval Shipyard. The city is converting much of the old shipyard into a business complex, industrial park, and distribution center.

The Continental Navy flag flies over Old Fort Mifflin (left) on Mud Island in the Delaware River. This was the site of the greatest bombardment of the American Revolution. Two hundred forty colonial defenders died during the seven-week siege. Pierre-Charles L'Enfant, the French engineer who later developed the city plan of the new national capital in Washington, directed the rebuilding of the fort. The City of Philadelphia restored the structure to its 1834 appearance. A not-for-profit corporation maintains the fort and offers walking tours of its moat, walls and gates, bastions, barracks, and hospital. The Passyunk Street Bridge offers an excellent view of the odiferous oil refineries (above) that were once a staple of, and an eyesore in, industrial Philadelphia.

Sculptor Joe Brown designed two football-player statues, including this punter (opposite)—as well as two baseball-player statues—that are mounted outside Veterans' Stadium in South Philadelphia. There are also hockey and basketball statues outside the Spectrum, the stadium's companion building in the sports complex. Outside the smaller arena, too, is Thomas Schomberg's bronze statue of Rocky Balboa (left), the hero of the series of Rocky boxing movies. In South Philly, too, is the colorful Mummers Museum (overleaf), which displays fascinating accoutrements and historical remnants of the annual New Years Day "Shooters' and Mummers' Parade." The first part of the spectacle's name derives from an early Swedish custom of firing off pistols and muskets to join with bells and noisemakers in heralding the new year.

45

Daly Street (opposite) is a quintessential lane of row houses in the Whitman neighborhood of South Philadelphia. Neighbors socialize outdoors as well as in each other's homes. Eateries like Jim's Steaks (left)—as in Philly cheesesteak hoagies, not filet mignon—and Lorenzo's Pizza Parlor (above) are part of the lively scene on eclectic South Street. The popular shopping corridor declined into tawdriness, but it has made such a comeback that South Street is often compared favorably with New York's Greenwich Village. Most shops, galleries, and restaurants—of which there are more than one hundred on this single short street—are open evenings, and the street is packed on weekends as well.

Four generations of the Ochs family meat business—three that are pictured (left)—have been prominent stall-holders at the Reading Terminal Market, which was beautifully refurbished in the early 1990s. Lena Zook (above), a young Amish woman from Lancaster County, serves fresh-baked soft pretzels—a time-honored Philadelphia delicacy—at another stand in the market. The last train to depart the old Reading Terminal upstairs (overleaf) pulled out on the evening of November 6, 1984, bound for Lansdale and carrying six hundred admirers of the old railroad and its flagship depot. The train shed was preserved and incorporated into the city's sweeping new Pennsylvania Convention Center.

More than 450,000 pieces form the collection of the Afro-American Historical and Cultural Museum (above), which focuses on the history of African Americans in Pennsylvania and the Delaware Valley, beginning with the arrival of the first African slaves in Philadelphia as early as 1639. The museum, which opened at Seventh and Arch streets in 1976 during the city's massive U.S. Bicentennial celebration, was founded with the express purpose of preserving the record of African-American contributions to society. Using materials donated by citizens of Tianjin, Philadelphia's sister city in the People's Republic of China, local Chinese artisans built the Chinese Friendship Gate (right)—the largest authentic Chinese gate outside China—straddling Tenth Street off Arch Street. More than fifty restaurants, and even a store devoted to fortune cookies, can be found in the city's modest Chinatown behind the gate.

In 1865, Philadelphia's Union League club—formed by wealthy donors to the Union cause in the Civil War—moved into a spacious Second Empire building (left), designed by John Fraser. The Philadelphia Academy of Music (above), which opened just before that war, is home to the nonpareil Philadelphia Orchestra. Architects Napoleon Le Brun and Gustave Runge modeled the academy after La Scala in Milan. Fanatical about acoustics, they directed that the building sit empty for a year, without a roof, so the walls could properly settle. Celebrated Philadelphia architect Frank Furness designed the building that houses the Pennsylvania Academy of Fine Arts (overleaf)—the nation's oldest art museum and school.

Owner-chef Georges
Perrier (above)
oversees Le Bec-Fin,
one of the nation's
most renowned restau-
rants. A meal at this
classic French estab-
lishment is an event
best planned—and
saved for—months in
advance. The elegant
dining room (right)
is one piece of the
palatial old Bellevue
Stratford Hotel that
survives in the restored
Hotel Atop the
Bellevue. After the

Bellevue Stratford
closed in 1986, ten
years following the
disastrous "Legion-
naires' Disease"
outbreak in the hotel,
the building was re-
habilitated as a retail
and office center
topped by a smaller
hotel. Kennedy Plaza
(overleaf) is one of
the sites of "Phillyfest,"
a series of free, noon-
time concerts and
other entertainment
that are a Philadel-
phia tradition.

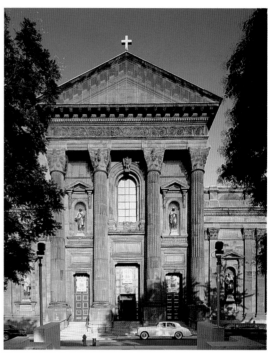

The gavel used to dedicate the corner- stone of Philadelphia's Masonic Temple (left)—one of the world's most impres- sive Masonic struc- tures—on June 24, 1868 was the one that George Washington, a Mason, had used to lay the cornerstone of the United States Capitol in Washing- ton seventy-five years earlier. One of the Philadelphia Masons' own, twenty-seven- year-old James

Windrim, designed the Norman structure. The interior features seven lodge halls— including an Egyptian Hall decorated with hieroglyphics copied from eight temples in Egypt—representing different periods in world history. The Cathedral of Saint Peter and Saint Paul (above), in grand Italian Renaissance style, was completed after twenty-two years of construction at Logan Square in 1888.

Claes Oldenburg designed the forty-five-foot-high Clothespin *(right) at Centre Square, across from City Hall. The sculpture was a radical departure from the traditionalist statuary abundant elsewhere in the city. Centre Square was one of five parks laid out by Philadelphia's original city planner, Thomas Holme. The others are Rittenhouse, Franklin, Logan, and Washington. Not since City Hall, at the turn of the twentieth century, and the PSFS Building, during the Great Depression of the 1930s, had both Philadelphia's skyline and its image so dramatically changed as they did when Willard G. Rouse's One and Two Liberty Place towers (opposite) rose in 1987 and 1990, respectively. The buildings broke the unofficial covenant against exceeding the 491-foot height of "Billy Penn's" hat atop City Hall.*

The 1910 Curtis Publishing Company Building (opposite), which housed the editors who produced the Ladies Home Journal, *features a series of stained-glass windows depicting milestones in communication. The building was extensively remodeled, converted into offices, and renamed Curtis Center in 1990. Rittenhouse Square's serene park (above) is surrounded by impressive brownstone apartments and office towers. The square is named for colonial astronomer David Rittenhouse. A "clothesline art" exhibit and a flower show are much-anticipated annual events in the park.*

While the skyline of Philadelphia has changed radically, with several soaring skyscrapers added in the 1990s, City Hall (left) has remained the focus of the Center City. The laborious restoration of City Hall in the late 1990s took years to reach many of the intricate details of this massive Second Empire struc- ture, including these Alexander Milne Calder sculptures (above) in a projected corner pavilion. Calder did not just design cherubs and other classical figures; he also executed the cher- ished twenty-seven- ton, bronze rendition of William Penn that stands atop the four-acre building.

Philadelphia has become a medley of shining skyscrapers and historic treasures. The William Penn statue (opposite) above the City Hall clock tower no longer has the highest aerie. The Schuylkill, the "River of Revolutions" (above), winds from the heart of Philadelphia to Valley Forge. Along the way are museums, mills and farmsteads, Revolutionary War forts, waterworks, limestone quarries, an industrial canal, a twenty-two-mile bikeway, and sites such as Mill Grove, the first American home of naturalist John J. Audubon. A plethora of museums, monuments, circles, and squares line the stately Benjamin Franklin Parkway (overleaf) connecting the Philadelphia Museum of Art and City Hall. "Philadelphia's Champs Elysées" was designed by French-born architects Jacques Greber and Paul Philippe Cret during the nation's effusive "City Beautiful" movement of the early twentieth century. Cret also designed another "Ben Franklin": the bridge over the Delaware River.

Logan Circle (opposite), began as one of William Penn's city squares that was turned into a traffic circle after World War I. It was named for James Logan, Philadelphia mayor, judge, mathematician, and land speculator, who administered Pennsylvania Colony for William Penn. Alexander Stirling Calder, son of the City Hall sculptor, designed Swann Memorial Fountain's bronze figures, which represent the city's three principal waterways: the Delaware and Schuylkill rivers, and Wissahickon Creek. Along the Benjamin Franklin Parkway, Auguste Rodin's statue The Thinker (left) announces the Rodin Museum, which exhibits many of the French artist's masterworks. The entryway was inspired by Chateau d'Issy—Rodin's own home in Meudon, France. The museum, a gift to the city from Jules Mastbaum, was dedicated a month after the Stock Market Crash of 1929.

An equestrian statue of George Washington (above), which stands on Eakins Oval before the Philadelphia Museum of Art, is one of more than twenty-five grand statues on the Benjamin Franklin Parkway. The monument, designed by German sculptor Rudolf Siemering, was originally placed in Fairmount Park in 1897 and moved to the parkway in 1928 as part of the effort by civic leaders to adorn Philadelphia in the trappings of a great world city. Herman Atkins MacNeil designed the marble pylons on the 1927 Civil War Soldiers and Sailors Memorial (right) at the entrance to the parkway. Battles from that war are inscribed on the memorial's walls that face the Museum of Art.

To discourage unsightly graffiti, Philadelphia commissioned street paintings such as this rendition of a Phillies' baseball game (above) under the Ridge Avenue Bridge, in locations that had been favorite targets of graffiti "taggers." The massive Cherry Hill Penitentiary (opposite)—officially known as the State Penitentiary for the Eastern District of Pennsylvania—on Fairmount Avenue in mid-city Philadelphia was built from 1822 to 1836 by John Haviland. Pioneering the stern "Pennsylvania System" of penology—linking solitary confinement with moral and vocational instruction—it became the model for more than five hundred other prisons worldwide. Both Alexis de Tocqueville and Charles Dickens visited America specifically to inspect the prison. Its thick granite walls, iron gratings, dark passageways, and seven cell blocks radiating from a central surveillance tower made it nearly escape-proof, to the relief of its neighbors. Closed in 1971, the old prison is now open for tours.

The Philadelphia Museum of Art (opposite) was built on Faire Mount Hill. Eli Kirk Price, who led the museum's fundraising drive, shrewdly directed that its two side wings be completed first, knowing that Philadelphians would not leave the central temple unbuilt. Its prodigious set of stairs is known around town as the "Rocky Stairs" because boxer Rocky Balboa, hero of the Rocky movie series, trained by ascending seventy-two of the ninety-nine steps. The museum displays its world-class collection—including a statue of Diana (above), created by sculptor Augustus Saint-Gaudens as a weathervane for the first Madison Square Garden in New York—in two hundred galleries. Downhill from the museum, along the Schuylkill River, is the Greek Revival-style Philadelphia Waterworks (overleaf). Designed by Frederick Graff, the building was the first steam pumping station of its kind in the nation.

One of Philadelphia's most beloved settings is the Victorian Boat House Row (above), illuminated at dusk and into the evening. Several of the structures, including one designed by famed Philadelphia architect Frank Furness, date to the late nineteenth century. Ten boat clubs—each with its coat of arms—comprise the "Schuylkill Navy" of rowers who keep their shells in the nineteenth-century boat houses and compete in regattas, including the largest intercollegiate race in the nation. There's even a "Frostbite Regatta" in November. The boat clubs compete according to levels of difficulty, so there's room for rowers of many abilities. Nine months a year, crews train on the Schuylkill (opposite)—which is Dutch for "hidden stream." Their shells may look simple and fragile, but they are expensive, costing as much as $10,000. Scullers were a favorite subject of Thomas Eakins, Philadelphia's master artistic realist.

Pine Breeze Villa (left) was designed as a model Japanese house by Junzō Yoshimura. It was built in 1953 in Nagoya, and presented by the American-Japan Society of Tokyo to the Museum of Modern Art for exhibition in New York in 1954. It was given to Philadelphia and reassembled in Fairmount Park with a garden designed by Tansai Sano that features traditional Japanese plants. The ninety-five-acre Laurel Hill Cemetery (above), overlooking the Schuylkill River, was the first graveyard in America to be planned by an architect—John Notman, in 1835. Originally, at least one specimen of every tree that could grow in Philadelphia's climate was planted here, which made Laurel Hill a popular nineteenth-century picnic and strolling spot.

Memorial Hall (opposite) in Fairmount Park was the Great Hall of the 1876 Centennial Exposition, which touted the young nation's industrial achievements. It and four other of the fair's halls were created by Hermann Schwartzmann, a Fairmount Park engineer who had never designed a building. Philadelphia's art museum was housed in Memorial Hall until the new museum opened in 1926. The winged horses (top right) flanking the building's entrance were created by Augustus Saint-Gaudens, who would later sculpt much of the statuary of the 1893 World's Columbian Exposition in Chicago. Fairmount Park is dotted with artistic delights like Frederic Remington's statue (bottom right). The park's Ellen Phillips Samuel Memorial Terrace (overleaf) along Kelly Drive was created in 1957 by sculptors, architects, and trustees of the park's art association.

90

Philadelphia judge Joyce Mozenter and her husband Bob, an eminent defense attorney, are inveterate joggers and two of the thousands of Philadelphians who savor Fairmount Park's wooded wonderland (above). At almost nine thousand acres, with more than one million trees and one hundred miles of nature trails, it is the world's largest landscaped urban park.

The red covered bridge, built in 1855, is the last covered bridge remaining within a large American city. The bronze lions (opposite) outside the Philadelphia Zoo are a favorite reconnoitering spot. Founded in 1859, the Zoological Society of Philadelphia was the first zoo in the nation, and its children's zoo, which opened in 1938, was also a first. So were the births of the first orangutans, chimpanzees, and cheetahs to be born in America. More than sixteen hundred animals live on the Philadelphia Zoo's forty-two acres today.

Thousands of commuters and Amtrak passengers board and arrive at 30th Street Station (opposite and above) in West Philadelphia each day. The monumental structure, completed in 1934 and beautifully restored in 1991, once even had a landing deck for small planes on its concrete roof. By locating the station across the Market Street Bridge over the Schuylkill River, the Pennsylvania Railroad deflected not just rail traffic, but also attention and urban development, away from Center City for the first time. The railroad turned to a Chicago architectural firm—Graham, Anderson, Probst, and White—to design the massive, neo-classical building. Because steam locomotives were fast fading from use, the architects were able to design the terminal above tracks, with smokeless electric trains in mind. The station's magnificent interior has been the setting for scenes in several movies, including Witness and Blow Out.

The University of Pennsylvania moved from downtown to West Philadelphia in 1870, but it was another twenty-five years before it had its first dormitory, the Quadrangle (opposite). The building, which is actually thirty-nine interconnecting structures around several courtyards, is rich in ornamentation, including its much-loved gargoyles. Long a men's dorm, the Quadrangle now houses approximately fourteen hundred undergraduates of both sexes. There are three statues of the school's founder, Benjamin Franklin, on the historic Ivy League campus. This 1899 bronze on a granite base (top left) was designed by John J. Boyle. In 1893, Philadelphia banker Anthony J. Drexel provided the seed money for the University City neighborhood's other center of higher education, the Drexel Institute of Art, Sciences, and Industry (bottom left), now Drexel University.

Most West Philadelphia row houses (above) are larger, more ornate, and architecturally more diverse than those in South Philadelphia, from which some in West Philly had moved. This was an early "streetcar suburb" where clerks, retail managers, lawyers, and other mid-level white-collar workers lived. Large Jewish and black enclaves grew up in West Philadelphia as well, and at the turn of the twentieth century, industrial Philadelphia had the largest African-American population of any northern city. Bartram's Garden (opposite) at Fifty-fourth Street and Lindbergh Boulevard in West Philadelphia is America's oldest botanical garden. The gardens surrounding the eighteenth-century home of John Bartram, considered the "father of American horticulture," include native trees, shrubs, and flowers gathered by Bartram himself. Plantings include the nation's oldest Ginkgo tree and a delicate Franklinia alatamaha, which Bartram named for his friend Benjamin Franklin.

Cliveden House (left) in Germantown showcases some of the finest furniture in Philadelphia. The house, on the site of the 1777 Revolutionary War Battle of Germantown, tells the story of generations of Philadelphia's Chew family. Colonial lawyer Benjamin Chew designed the elegant Georgian mansion himself, with help from a local master carpenter.

The Chew family lived in the house until 1972, when they gave it to the National Trust for Historic Preservation. Germantown's Ebenezer Maxwell Mansion (above), completed in 1859, was owned by a prominent dry-goods merchant and land speculator. The Victorian house combines several styles, and much of its exterior wood is painted to resemble stone.

ROLL OF HONOR

Germantown's Monument to Heroes Dead *in the Civil War (opposite) was unveiled in 1883. Memorial tablets list fallen Union soldiers and sailors from the* city's Germantown ward. *In Chestnut Hill, the highest point in Philadelphia, stands Chestnut Hill Academy (above). Built in 1884, it was once the Wissahickon* Inn, *an in-city retreat for Philadelphians. Shipping executive Henry Howard Houston opened the inn to entice city dwellers to visit the housing development* he was erecting in *Chestnut Hill. Surrounded by a porch, the inn offered 250 rooms. Houston was also a director of the Pennsylvania Railroad, and he con-* vinced the line to *extend into his development. From there, it would reach to Paoli in the suburbs and help create the fashionable "Main Line."*

Ropsley (right) was designed in 1916 as a small country estate on four acres in Chestnut Hill. It declined over the decades before architect John P. A. Todd orchestrated a meticulous restoration in the early 1990s. The estate's allée of lindens (above) represents Danaüs's fifty mythological daughters, all but one of whom slew their husbands at the command of their father. The forty-nine were doomed to forever draw water with a sieve in Hades. Manayunk (overleaf), a vibrant shopping enclave, was once a thriving mill town. Schuylkill River water power drove spinning wheels at so many cotton and wool mills that Manayunk was known as the "Lowell of Pennsylvania."

The name for Manayunk (left), once a textile-mill town high above the Schuylkill River, was taken from the Indian word meaning "place where we go to drink." Philadelphians still do now that restored Manayunk has become an enclave of shops, restaurants, and pubs. The 1859 Italianate Ryerss Victorian Mansion (above) in Fox Chase's Burholme Park was the home of Joseph W. Ryerss, a shipping executive whose love for animals led to his founding of a veterinary infirmary. The house, with its extensive Asian furnishings, is now a public museum and free library. The 1720 Logan Inn (overleaf) in New Hope is the second-oldest inn in quaint Bucks County—and one of the oldest in continuous operation in the nation. It was once the Ferry Inn, hosteling passengers—including George Washington as many as five times—planning to take the ferry across the Delaware River.

In 1892, architect Horace Trumbauer completed his first great assignment: the medieval-style home (above) of sugar refinery owner William Welsh Harrison in rural Glenside. Called Grey Towers for its locally quarried gray marble, the grandiose building—based on Alnwick Castle, historic seat of the dukes of Northumberland in England—was one of the largest homes in the country. It is now the principal hall of Beaver College. Frank Lloyd Wright designed Beth Shalom Synagogue (right) in Elkins Park in 1959–60. Up to one thousand congregants worship in an upstairs temple beneath a translucent, pyramid-shaped roof symbolic of Mount Sinai.

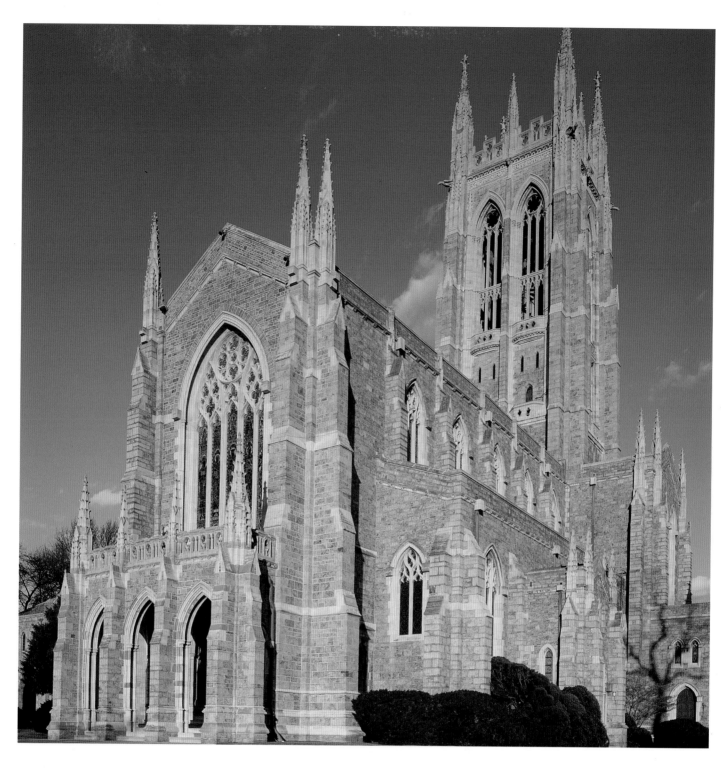

The 1883 Saint Thomas of Villanova Church (opposite) is on the Villanova University campus, but it is a parish church, not the university chapel. Much of the funding for its construction came from Irish Catholic immigrants working in the hotels and summer homes of prominent Philadelphia families. Building of the Church of New Jerusalem's Bryn Athyn Cathedral (above), overlooking the Pennypack Valley, began in 1914 and continued for several decades using the painstaking medieval guild system of construction. Longwood Gardens (overleaf), established by Pierre S. Du Pont in Kennett Square near Brandywine, is one of the world's most spectacular horticultural displays. More than eleven thousand plants can be found within Longwood's 1,050 outdoor acres and 20 indoor gardens.

Index

A big Columbus Day festival assembles each year near the statue of the great Italian navigator in South Philadelphia's Marconi Park. Saint Mary Magdalen de Pazzi, the nation's first Italian church, was founded in Philadelphia in 1852, and some tensions developed as the area evolved from being a primarily Irish neighborhood into a largely Italian and Jewish one.